troubleshoot
PC problems
yourself

Anthony Price

Hodder Education
338 Euston Road, London NW1 3BH.

Hodder Education is an Hachette UK company

First published in UK 2011 by Hodder Education.

This edition published 2011.

10 9 8 7 6 5 4 3 2 1

The publisher has used its best endeavours to ensure that any website
addresses referred to in this book are correct and active at the time of going
to press. However, the publisher and the author have no responsibility for the
websites and can make no guarantee that a site will remain live or that the
content will remain relevant, decent or appropriate.

The publisher has made every effort to mark as such all words which it
believes to be trademarks. The publisher should also like to make it clear that
the presence of a word in the book, whether marked or unmarked, in no way
affects its legal status as a trademark.

Every reasonable effort has been made by the publisher to trace the copyright
holders of material in this book. Any errors or omissions should be notified in
writing to the publisher, who will endeavour to rectify the situation for any
reprints and future editions.

Hachette UK's policy is to use papers that are natural, renewable and
recyclable products and made from wood grown in sustainable forests.
The logging and manufacturing processes are expected to conform to the
environmental regulations of the country of origin.

www.hoddereducation.co.uk

Typeset by MPS Limited, a Macmillan Company.
Printed in Great Britain by CPI Cox & Wyman, Reading.

Contents

1

maintaining
Windows

Windows is the name of the operating system software that makes the collection of hardware that you can see in front of you into a working computer. Without an operating system, all you have is a collection of parts.

In order to keep your system functioning properly Windows needs to be maintained; just as you check the oil in the car or mow the lawn from time to time, there are tasks that need to be carried out on your PC or laptop. Fortunately, Windows provides the tools to do this operating system maintenance easily. In this chapter we will look at four of the most useful tools that come with the current Windows version – Windows 7. We will also consider a special mode of Windows operation – Safe Mode – that will give you access to other repair and recovery tools.

Windows versions

This book is written in terms of Windows 7 Home Premium Edition; this is the most frequently used version of Windows for home users. The book assumes that you are familiar with the basics of using Windows. If you are not, or you need a primer on Windows 7 – try *Teach Yourself Get Started in Windows 7*.

Windows 7

Windows 7 comes in several different versions, some of which are only available in certain territories, for licensing and legal reasons. For most of us the choices are between:

* Windows 7 Home Premium
* Windows 7 Professional
* Windows 7 Ultimate

These are available in both 32-bit and 64-bit versions. A 32-bit version will run on a 64-bit processor, but a 64-bit version will not run on a 32-bit processor.

System requirements for running Windows 7 are:

* 1 gigahertz (GHz) or faster 32-bit (×86) or 64-bit (×64) processor
* 1 gigabyte (GB) RAM (32-bit) or 2 GB RAM (64-bit)
* 16 GB available hard disk space (32-bit) or 20 GB (64-bit)
* Direct × 9 graphics device with WDDM 1.0 or higher driver.

Windows Vista

Windows Vista is the immediate forerunner of Windows 7. The hardware requirements to run it are only slightly less than Windows 7 so an upgrade is probably feasible. If you are considering an upgrade there is an upgrade advisor tool that can be downloaded from:

http://www.microsoft.com/windows/windows-7/get/upgrade-advisor.aspx

If you don't want to upgrade to Windows 7 you will find that most of the features in this book will work if you are using Vista.

Windows XP

XP is now a 'mature' system. Consequently it lacks many of the advanced features of the later versions. However, if you are still using XP, many of the features in this book will work, though you may have to do a bit of head scratching and puzzling before you get a result.

Four things you can do now

PC systems tend to slow down through time for various reasons. Moreover, they are often set up to give the most attractive appearance at the expense of performance, and this can be significant if you have an older or relatively low-powered PC.

Before you start, consider the safety and integrity of your data. The tools you are about to use are safe and reliable and have been in use by millions of users for many years. However, things do go wrong very occasionally. For example, a mains power failure part way through a disk defragmentation could cause data loss or corruption.

As a rule, it is wise to back up data and make a note of settings before doing any maintenance work. Having backed up your data (or decided to accept the small risk of not doing so) we can get down to business with the operating system tools.

Note: some of the utilities on some systems may require you to have Administrator rights to use them. If, when you try to access a utility, you receive an error message along the lines of 'You do not have sufficient rights to ...' Right-click on the program icon and select 'Run as Administrator' from the context menu.

The following are the four most useful tools in Windows 7 that can help with your maintenance tasks:

Check Disk

Like many Windows utilities, Check Disk can be accessed through several routes. Space limitations mean that it is not possible to describe them all here. Perhaps the easiest way is to select the disk you wish to check, then select from the Tools menu. To run Check Disk:

1 Click (or double-click) on **Computer** (right-hand side of the Start menu).
2 Right-click on the C: drive and select **Properties**.
3 Select the **Tools** tab.
4 Click **Check Now**.

The following figure shows the Check Disk utility. Click **Start** to begin. If you leave the two option boxes unchecked, Check Disk will simply check the file system for errors. More thorough testing can be done by selecting either or both of the checkboxes. Depending on the choice you make, you may have to restart the machine. If you do this, the disk will be checked as the PC starts up and you will see a (probably unfamiliar) text-based screen – white characters on a blue screen – which will report progress and, when complete, continue the boot process to the usual Desktop.

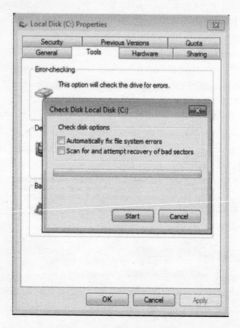

The Disk Cleanup Wizard

Hard disks accumulate rubbish files through time — temporary files from application installers and the Internet are probably the worst culprits. These files take up disk space and, especially if the disk is fairly full, can slow the system down substantially. The Disk Cleanup Wizard is the Windows utility to deal with these unwanted files and it is available in all Windows versions.

1 Click on **My Computer**.
2 Right-click on the C: drive and select **Properties**.
3 Select the **General** tab.
4 Click **Disk** Cleanup.

The system will spend a few seconds gathering information and will then present you with some options.

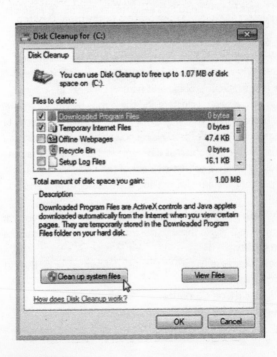

(Note the button for Clean up system files.)

5 Accept the default values, or change them by checking or
unchecking boxes.

6 When you have made your choices click **OK**. You will be
asked 'Are you sure you want to permanently delete these
files?' – Click the **Delete Files** button if you do.

The system will then display its progress and offer the option
to cancel until it is finished.

The Disk Defragmenter

Imagine a library where returned books are placed on the
first available shelf space and the catalogue is updated to
record their new position. After a while, books would be shelved
all over the place, and something like a multi-volume encyclopaedia
would take a long time to find because the individual volumes
would be on different shelves or even different floors of the
building.

Windows stores files rather like the books in the library
example. When a file is written to the hard disk it is written
to the first available storage unit (cluster). A large file may be
written across several clusters and these may be widely separated.
When files are deleted it makes more clusters available, possibly
in the middle of other files. This is known as fragmentation and
the answer to the problem is defragmentation: that is, rearranging
the storage clusters so that all parts of the same file are on the
same part of the hard disk, making them easier to find and quicker
to load.

As with many utilities and programs in Windows 7 you can use
the 'traditional' route through the menu system or you can use the
Search facility.

For example, navigate to the disk defragmenter by the
traditional route:

1 Right-click on **Computer**.

2 Right-click on the C: Drive.

3 Select **Properties > Tools**.

4 Click the **Defragment now** button.

Alternatively, type 'defragment' in to the Search box on the **Start** menu and select the Defragmentation utility from the list.

Whichever route you choose you will see a panel which looks like this:

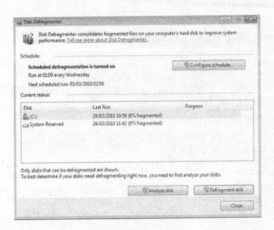

As you can see from the figure, there are three buttons: **Configure schedule, Analyze disk** and **Defragment disk**.

* **Configure schedule.** If you click on the **Configure schedule** button you will be presented with a dialog box that gives you the tools to schedule a regular defragmentation session.

* **Analyze disk.** This option calculates the level of fragmentation of the disk and recommends that you carry out a defrag if the level of defragmentation warrants it.

* **Defragment disk.** This carries out a defragmentation irrespective of the level of fragmentation on the disk.

Defragmentation of a large disk can be a time-consuming business. You can continue working as the defrag utility works in the background but this will slow things down even further so there is case to be made for setting up a regular schedule – to run at a time when the machine is on but not in use – and forget about it.

Visual Effects

Windows is designed to be visually attractive, with 3-D buttons, sliding or fading menus and other visual effects. If you like these features and you have a reasonably powerful machine to support them, fine. However, if you want to release some processing power you can modify these special effects through the Windows interface.

To change the visual effects settings:

1 Right-click on **Computer** and select **Properties** from the context menu.
2 Click on the **Change Settings** link near the bottom right of the page.
3 Select the **Advanced** tab.
4 Click on the first **Settings** button (the one under the heading of Performance).

The following figure shows the Visual Effects settings in Windows 7. They are set to the default value of **Let Windows Choose** and in this instance it has chosen settings which are the same as the **Best Appearance** settings. Selecting **Best Performance** will disable all of the visual effects. **Custom settings** allows you to choose the combination of visual effects that you want by checking or unchecking the appropriate boxes. The best way to decide what you want is simply to experiment. If you don't like the results, you can always change them back!

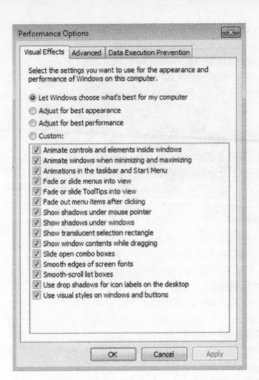

Using Safe Mode

Safe Mode is a special diagnostic mode of Windows which loads and runs the operating system with the minimum of drivers. It is sometimes possible to boot to Safe Mode when a machine won't otherwise start. The easiest way to start Safe Mode is to hold down [F8] as the system boots up. This takes you to Windows' Advanced Boot Options:

At this screen, select **Safe Mode** and press [Enter]. The system
will continue to run in white on black text mode and you can watch
the drivers being loaded. This may take a while.

When all drivers are loaded you will be presented with a
graphical desktop.

Note that Windows displays the Help file for Safe Mode on
the right of the Desktop and that the corners of the display show
the words 'Safe Mode' to remind you that this is not a normal
working mode.

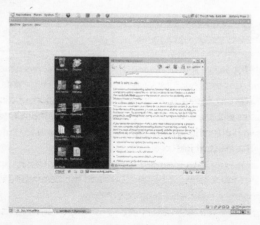

Once you are in Safe Mode you can fix any problems that may be hindering the normal boot process such as incorrect display settings or corrupted drivers. When you have finished simply reboot as normal.

Using the Repair your Computer option

If you cannot fix your problems by using Safe Mode there is a Repair option in the Advanced Boot menu which requires you to select a language-specific keyboard and to log in using your password. If you do this you will be presented with the **System Recovery** options.

* **Startup Repair** is an automated repair option. Clicking on this will cause Windows to attempt to repair itself without any further input from you.
* The **System Restore** options are described in Chapter 2.
* The **Windows Memory Diagnostic** utility checks for hardware faults in system RAM and the **Command Prompt** opens a command-prompt Window.

With luck you may never need to use any of these tools.

2
backups

Windows provides tools for backing up your data and – behind the scenes – it backs up system settings and information so that you can restore your system with the System Restore utility if you have problems.

In the event of a problem that makes your system unbootable from its hard disk you can boot from a Repair Disk. You need to make this *before* you run into problems.

In this chapter, we will look at Repair Disks, the Windows Backup utility and how to restore your system using the System Restore utility.

The material presented in this chapter is sufficient for the needs of most home users, but there's a lot more to explore if you are interested or feel that you need more sophisticated tools and techniques.

Repair Disks

Windows 7 provides a number of backup tools which means that you can back up your data, your settings, or even your entire installed system. Obviously, there is no point in having a backup unless you have the means to restore it and one of the tools for restoring a system is a Repair Disk. This is a bootable CD which provides much the same facilities as Safe Mode/Repair option (see Chapter 1) on a system that is otherwise unbootable. The utility to make a Repair Disk is part of the backup system. As with many features in Windows there is more than one way of starting it:

Either: Click on Control Panel in the **Start** menu and navigate to System and **Security > Backup your computer > Create a system repair disk**

Or: type 'backup' in the Search box on the **Start** menu and select from the results

Or: type 'repair' in the Search box on the **Start** menu and select from the results.

Making a Repair Disk

For this, you will need a blank, writeable CD and a working CD drive.

1 Start the Create Repair Disk utility. You will see a dialog box that looks like this:

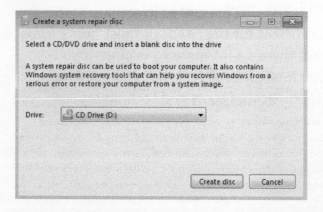

2 Put a blank writeable CD in the drive and click on the
Create disc button. The system will take a couple of
minutes to prepare the necessary files and burn them to
the CD that you have provided. When it has finished you
will see something like:

3 Label the disk and store it somewhere safe. With luck you
may never need it but it is as well to be prepared.

Repair Disks are not specific to the systems on which they are
made but if you have both 32-bit and 64-bit systems you should
make a separate version for each type.

Backups

A backup is simply a copy of some files that exists
independently of the system on which they were made and which
can be restored if the originals are lost or corrupted. Whether you
back up user files or the entire system, whether the medium is
CD/DVD or a hard disk, the backup should be stored securely as far
away as possible from the system itself, ideally in a different room
or even a different building. We will consider only 'local' media but
the techniques outlined in this chapter can also be used over a
network.

Setting up the Backup utility

This only needs to be done once, though you can, of course, change the settings later if you wish. To set up the backup system, open the Backup utility. You will see something like this:

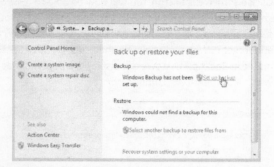

1 Click on the **Set up backup** link. Windows will search for suitable media and list them. This will include removable media such as writeable CDs/DVDs or hard disks which may be removable or fixed inside the PC. Obviously for a backup, a removable hard disk is better than built-in, but built-in is better than nothing.

2 Choose your Backup Destination from the list.

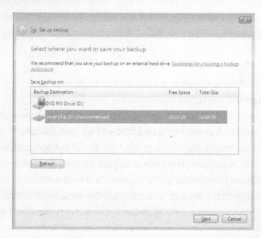

3 At the next stage you will be asked what you want to back up. The default is to let Windows decide and for most of us this is a sensible choice. It will back up your user files ignoring temporary files, program files, etc.

4 Click on the **Next** button. You will now be able to review your choices. Note the option to **Edit the Schedule**. This should be set to perform a backup (say) once a week so that you can set and forget it. When you have finished click on **Save Settings and Run Backup**. Windows will display a progress bar as it works and confirm its completion.

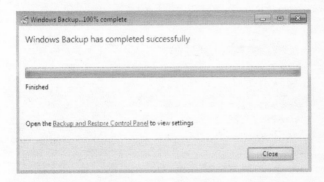

From now on Windows will perform a backup according to your specification and schedule until you decide to change things.

Restoring from backup

This is essentially the reverse of the backup process.

1 Start the Backup utility.

2 Select the files and folders that you want to restore – all users, all your own files or selected files and folders.

3 Having made your choices click on the **Next** button. You will now be given the option to restore files to their original location (the default) or to choose a new location.

4 Having made your choice, click on the **Restore** button. If there are any conflicts between files the system will inform you and you can choose what to do about them.

Note the checkbox – bottom left – which enables you to automate your responses.

5 Once you have told the system how to resolve any conflicts it will run to completion without further user intervention.

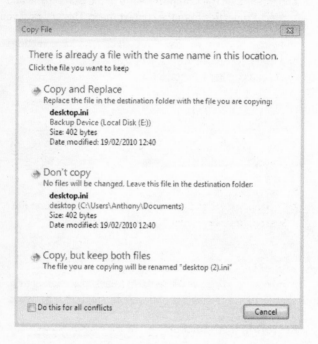

System Restore

System Restore is concerned only with system files. Its operation is the same in all Windows versions. Word processing files, pictures, e-mails and other data files are not affected by this utility. This means that you need to back these items up for yourself using the Backup utility that comes with Windows or by one of the alternatives. The good side of this is that if you do need to 'roll back' your system to an earlier date, you won't lose your data.

Restoring your system

There are several routes to the System Restore utility. You can navigate to the Control Panel by searching on 'restore' through the Start menu or like this:

1 Right-click on the **Computer** entry in the **Start** menu and select **Properties** from the context menu. This will take you to part of the Control Panel:

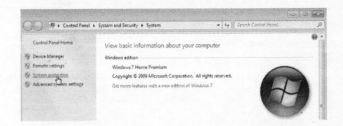

2 Click on the link to **System Protection**, then click on the **System Restore** button. This displays a panel:

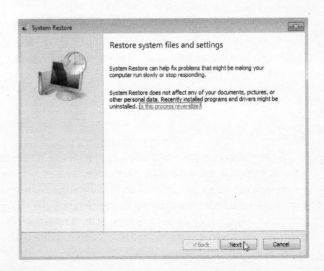

3 Click on **Next**. Windows will now list the available restore points.

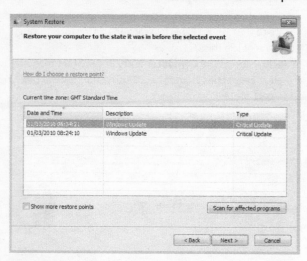

Note that there are options to show other restore points and to check the impact of using a particular restore point on your installed programs.

4 When you have established which restore point is best for your needs (usually the most recent one) click on the **Next** button. You will then be prompted to confirm your restore point. Click on **Finish**. You will then be presented with a final warning:

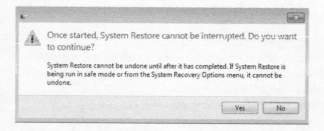

5 Click on the **Yes** button to proceed. Windows will now start the shut-down process.

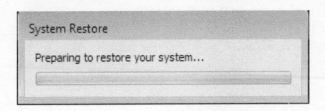

6 Windows will reboot and output progress messages as the Restore process proceeds. When it is finished you will be presented with the usual login procedures (or none if your system is set up that way). Finally, Windows will confirm the Restoration.

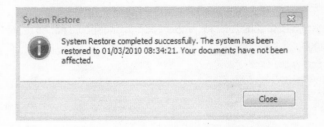

7 Click on **Close** and continue using your restored system.

Shadow copies

Every time that Windows makes a restore point it also makes shadow copies of your user files. This means that you can restore an individual user file from the Restore system.

1 Right-click on the file icon and select **Restore previous versions** from the context menu.

2 This will list previous versions of the file that have been
saved as part of the restore points. Click on the old version
that you require — there's only one in this example — and it
will be restored.

Useful though it may be in an emergency, the Shadow copy
system is no substitute for proper backups and should not be relied
upon.

Things to remember

* A backup is simply a copy of some files which exists independently of the system where they were created. Useful though they may be, shadow copies on your system are not independent.
* Techniques outlined in this chapter have been illustrated by reference to local disks and storage. They apply equally well to a network system.
* A Repair Disk is bootable. A system image disk (or disk set) is not.
* You can set your own restore points in addition to those created by Windows.
* You can remove unwanted restore points to save space and improve performance.
* You can locate a program – such as Backup – by typing its name in the Search box on the **Start** menu.
* You an add a program to the **Start** menu or the Taskbar by right-clicking on its name and choosing the appropriate option from the context menu.
* Because the entries in the **Start** menu and Taskbar are shortcuts you can remove them without affecting the installed programs.

3

Control
Panel

The Control Panel pulls together utilities that range from the simple – like changing the system time and date – to advanced tools that are likely to be of interest only to system administrators and power users. As with many things in computing the best way of learning is by having a go.

In this chapter we will look at how the Control Panel works (basically it is indexed on keywords) and step through a straightforward example of setting the system date and time. Once you have done this and developed a feel for how the system works, you can spend as much (or as little) time as you like exploring it. Remember that no matter how deep you go into its structure you are never more than a couple of mouse clicks away from Control Panel 'Home'.

The Control Panel has been a feature of Windows systems over several editions. The version that is part of Windows 7 is the most comprehensive to date. If you click on the Control Panel entry in the Start menu you will see something like this:

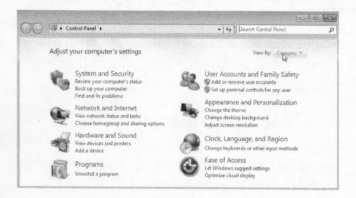

This is the Windows default 'Category view'. At the top right corner there is a Search box which means that you can search for any item within the Control Panel. The search engine uses keywords rather than program names. For instance if you type 'backup' in the search box you will see:

Note that the search has identified not just the backup program, but associated topics such as Restore and System Restore. There is also a link to the wider Windows Help system.

There are Back and Forward arrows (top left) and a drop-down list of previous locations:

If you switch from the default Category View to one of the icon views you will see a full list of Control Panel items which you can click and use. Some people prefer this view; it is really just a matter of what suits your way of working.

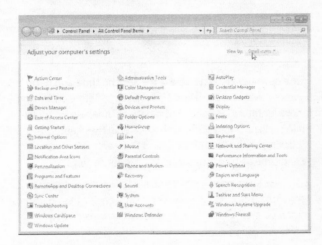

This figure shows the Small Icon View of the Control Panel. Whichever view you prefer (and you can swap between them as you wish) the icon view gives a good indication of the range of utilities that Windows provides.

How the Control Panel works

Because the Control Panel is indexed on key words there are many cross-references within its structure. This supports a task-oriented approach to using it. For example, if you wish to change the time shown by the system clock you could search the Control Panel for the word 'time'.

The Control Panel search utility in action

Search term: 'time'. Results:

The obvious candidate here is the **Set the time and date** entry under the main **Date and Time** heading. Before clicking on this, note for future reference the variety of Time-related topics listed. We will return to some of these later in the chapter.

Clicking on the **Set the time and Date** entry opens the Date and Time panel which shows the current settings.

Clicking on the **Change Date and Time** button opens another panel which provides the tools to do this.

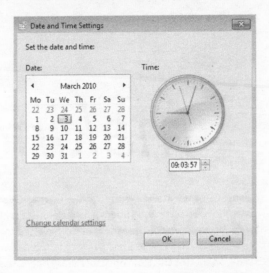

Make your changes – or click on **Cancel** if you are just exploring – and you will return to the main Date and Time panel. Note that there are also options to change the time zone and to enable (or disable) daylight saving. Note, too, that there are additional tabs for setting up additional clocks and synchronizing your system time with an Internet time server.

Exploring the Control Panel

Now that you know how the Control Panel works and how to change between Category and Icon views of its contents you can explore the utilities that if offers. The system is too big to catalogue all of it here and some advanced features are mainly of interest to System Administrators.

4

making a support call

With just a little knowledge and persistence you can achieve a lot in terms of making your PC work properly but at some stage you may need to ask for help from a Help Desk or a PC technician.

The key to making a successful call – that is, a call that is brief and effective – is to know the sorts of detail that the Help Desk will ask and to have the details to hand. You don't need to wait until you have problems in order to do this, so this chapter will explain what information you need and where to find it. We will also look at how to prepare for making a call and how to find – and judge the value of – a PC technician.

Before you call for Help

Sooner or later you will need to make a support call to a Help Desk or look through the phone book or the small ads to find a PC technician. Either of those options will cost you money, so before you do anything, read this chapter.

Whether you are going to tackle the problem yourself or call in an outsider – Help Desk or technician – the first thing to do is to arm yourself with the facts after you have rebooted the machine.

There are two reasons for this. First, simply closing the system down and restarting it cures a lot of transient faults. The contents of RAM (main system memory) are lost in the shutdown and reloaded from scratch when you start up again. Second, if you haven't rebooted, almost any Help Desk or technician will ask if you have done this, so why pay an expert to tell you this when you can simply do it yourself?

If the reboot doesn't work then you need to define the problem. The Help Desk operator or technician will ask you what the problem is and the clearer you are in your description the less time (and money) you will spend on a support call. Indeed, preparing to make a succinct fault report is often the first step to fixing the problem yourself. Describing – or preparing to describe – something to someone else can be a very effective way of organizing your own thinking.

Defining the problem

This need not be formal or complicated. What is necessary is to describe what happens or fails to happen. For example, 'I can't connect to the Internet' needs to be fleshed out a bit in order to be useful. Are you using a dialup modem connection or broadband? What, exactly do you do which causes the problem to manifest itself? A better description may be something like: 'When I click on the Internet Explorer icon on my Desktop, the modem begins to dial then, after half a minute I get an error message "remote host not responding"'.

A description along those lines makes it clear that the problem is with a dialup connection and suggests that the problem is probably with your Internet Service Provider – possibly their server is down for some reason.

Your best bet, in that scenario, would be simply to wait for an hour or two and try again later. Or, if you are in a hurry for a result, phone the ISP or use someone else's system to check the ISP's status page on the Web to see if there is a known problem. The following figure shows part of a status page from a UK-based ISP.

The support page gives details of known problems and provides a link to further Help. The same information could probably have been obtained through a single brief phone call to the ISP.

Service	Status		Next Update
Hosted Exchange:		Monitoring	05/03/10 15:00
Broadband:		Planned Maintenance	
Business Mobile:		Working	
Data/PC Backup:		Working	
Dial Up:		Working	
E-Store:		Working	
Email:		Working	

Gathering the information

Whoever you call for help, they will want to know the key facts about your system. It will save you time (and money) to have these facts to hand, so document them before you need them. Write them down and keep a print of the information somewhere safe. There's not much point in having your system details stored on a system that has stopped working! The information that you need might look something like that in Table 4.1.

You could extend this list almost indefinitely or gather more detail if you need or want it. A look at System Information in the Control Panel will give a lot more detail.

Table 4.1

Item	Details	Source
PC manufacturer	DNUK	Documentation that came with the system Manufacturer's badge on case
CPU	AMD Athlon XP 2000 running at 1.67 GHz	Control Panel: System
Installed RAM	4 Gb	Control Panel: System
Operating System	Windows 7 Home Premium	Control Panel: System
Disk Storage		
Hard Disk 1 Drive C:	20 Gb capacity with 10.6 Gb of free space NTFS File System	Properties of Computer – right-click on drive icon
Hard Disk 2 Drive F:	9.99 Gb capacity with 9.90 Gb free space NTFS File System	Properties of Computer – right-click on drive icon
Drives with removable storage	3.5" floppy drive 1 CD writer 1 DVD writer	Properties of Computer – right-click on drive icon or look at the front of the case!

Other useful information are e-mail and ISP login details. You will need to know/find out:

Table 4.2

Item	Details
ISP	UKLINUX
Dialup Number	08459042086
User Name	elenmar
Password	********
Incoming Mail Server	pop3.elenmar.com
Outgoing Mail Server	smtp.elenmar.com
Password	********

Passwords

Write them down if you must, but NEVER tell anyone your password over the phone or by e-mail. If absolutely necessary, a password can be reset at your supplier's end. If this is necessary, log in as soon as possible afterwards and change it to something that is easy for you to remember but is hard for someone else to guess. It is good practice to use a mixture of upper and lower-case letters and numbers for a password, e.g. 'Fr1day' is an easy to remember variant on 'friday' – easy to remember but hard to guess (at least, it was until somebody put it in a book!)

To find your user name for your Internet connection, just click on the icon that you generally use to connect to the Internet. The following figure shows details of an ADSL modem connection.

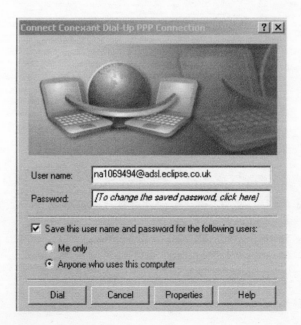

Your mail server settings can be obtained from your mail program. The standard mail client for Windows 7 is Windows Live Mail.

To find the settings for that program:

1 Click on the **Windows Live Mail** entry in the **Start** menu.
2 Right-click on the name of your mail account in the **Live Mail** menu, then select Properties from the context menu.
3 Select the **Servers** tab.

4 If – and only if – the box labelled **My Server Requires Authentication** is ticked (as in the figure), you need to click **Settings** which will take you to a further screen where you can enter separate account details and password for your outgoing mail server. Most home users will not need to do this.

If you are not using Windows Live Mail, the procedure for finding the information you require is much the same in other mail clients such as Eudora or Thunderbird.

Calling the Help Desk

Many of the large high street retailers offer some sort of warranty or support deal as part of the package. Typically, this requires you to call a Help Desk who will talk you through your problems. These calls are often expensive premium numbers so the more organized you are before you make the call the less it will cost.

Perhaps the most important thing is to have details of the system – make, model number, etc. – to hand along with details of any support contract or warranty you may have. With this in place, dial the number for the Help Desk, describe the problem to the operator and attempt to find a solution together.

Most Help Desk operators are helpful and knowledgeable about their own company's products and will talk you through the process of fixing things. However, they are usually working from a script and can only address a fairly limited range of problems. If, between you, you can't fix a problem fairly quickly, they may suggest running a Restore Disk – usually on one or two bootable CDs – which will restore the system to its original factory settings. Such a restore will destroy all of your data, and installed programs and settings. It may well fix your problem or, if it doesn't, it will have restored the factory defaults so that the Help Desk are now dealing with a machine whose configuration is known to them in detail.

Finding a PC technician

Not everyone has a system which is covered by a warranty or a support contract so, if you can't fix the problem yourself,

you will need to find a PC technician to do the job for you.
There are three main sources of help for PC problems:

* high street names
* local computer companies
* sole traders – freelance technicians.

The high street names

These are the sort of household names that advertise on
television and in national newspapers. Most of them offer support
and extended warranty services for equipment bought from them.
They also accept work from non-customers, but generally require
you to take your PC to their premises or charge a hefty premium for
a call out to your home. Their hourly rates are generally something
like double those of the small local operator. The advantage of
dealing with these companies is that they will (probably) still be
there next year and that they have a reputation which they care
about. They tend to do a good, if somewhat expensive, job. However,
they are usually keen to try to sell you upgrades and extras that you
may not really need.

A typical offer from one of these chains consists of doing
the work – even if it's only a 'PC Health Check' for the quoted
price – then advising that the machine 'could benefit from
more RAM' and offering to fit it free if you pay for it while they
still have the PC in their workshop. It's a fact of course, that just
about any PC could benefit from more RAM – it's one of the
most cost-effective upgrades that you can do yourself. A stick
or two can be fitted in minutes and you can buy them online.
The price from one of the high street retailers is generally
something like 30% more than you would pay for it online from
the manufacturer: no wonder they can afford to spend two minutes
fitting it 'free'.

Local computer companies

A look through Yellow Pages or a local directory such as Thomson
will generally list several local computer companies. These vary in

size and the services they can offer. Like the high street names they will probably advertise that their staff have various qualifications (more on qualifications later). The fact that they are in a directory indicates that they are established. They can offer the same advantages as their larger counterparts along with the same shortcomings – higher prices and trying to sell you upgrades you don't really need.

Sole traders

These independent operators will probably give you a better price than the larger companies, mainly because they have lower overheads. Most of them work from home or from small rented premises. When you buy from the high street or the commercial/business park you are paying your share of the costs of the business rates, not to mention the costs of the glitzy premises.

The independent operators, at their best, can offer you a personal service in your own home for about half the price of the bigger companies. Many of them are skilled and experienced PC technicians; often they are employed in a school or a local authority and do a certain amount of freelance work as a sideline. A handful, though, are cyber cowboys, rip-off artists and clowns. So how do you know which is which?

Word-of-mouth recommendation from satisfied local customers is the best possible indication that someone is competent. If someone known to you can say 'Fred Bloggs did a good job for me' then there's a strong case for hiring Fred to do a job for you.

If no one you know can recommend a technician, then look in the small ads in the local paper or even the postcards in the newsagent's windows or notice boards in a local college. Before making the initial approach, consider the advert. Does it give an address and a landline number, or just a name and a mobile number? Does it say anything about qualifications, the services offered? Does the technician offer a 'no fix, no fee' service?

Having chosen perhaps two or three local techs, phone them and have a chat. Describe your problem in outline and ask if they can help. Ask what their hourly rate is, above all ask if they can give you names and contact details of (say) three local customers for whom they have worked in the past six months. And follow up on this. If you are dealing with a reputable, competent business there won't be a problem in obtaining and checking on customer references.

Qualifications

Qualifications are no substitute for ability and experience, but they do matter. The basic qualification for a PC technician is the A+ Certificate from the Computing Technology Industry Association (CompTIA). CompTIA is a Chicago-based organization with members in 102 countries. Its corporate members include global household names like Intel and Microsoft. The A+ Certification is gained by taking two rigorous online examinations designed to test the knowledge of a PC technician with a minimum of six months' work experience. The examinations test the technician's knowledge of hardware, operating systems and the basics of networking. The content of the exams is updated every couple of years to reflect changes in the actual work carried out by CompTIA certified technicians who are working in the field. (Details of all CompTIA qualifications can be seen at their website www.comptia.org.)

There are other higher qualifications from companies such as Microsoft and Novell, but these are specific to those companies' own products. There are also, of course, various academic qualifications up to and including Master's degrees in information technology or computing. However, for a practical working tech, earning his or her living in the trade, CompTIA Certified PC Support Technician is about the best badge there is.

Things to remember

* Always reboot your PC before trying to diagnose a fault.
* Make (and keep up to date) a record of all your system settings. Keep copies away from your PC.

* Define the problem. If you can describe it accurately you are halfway to solving it!
* Have all your settings information available before you call the Help Desk. It will make your call shorter, more effective and cheaper.
* When choosing a PC technician look for someone with CompTIA A+ Certification and (preferably) some satisfied local customers.

5

inside the box

Looking after your hardware is usually a simple matter of replacing like with like components or adding a component to an existing expansion slot. This chapter takes you through the process of opening the case and handling the components without damaging them (or yourself) in the process. It also helps you to identify the main components on your system and the types of cables and connectors that they use. We look at the process of replacing or upgrading some key components such as disk drives or PCI cards and consider why *some* components are not worth upgrading.

Note: If you intend to work through this chapter as a hands-on practical you *may* find it useful to buy (and use) an anti-static wrist strap.

Working safely

Modern hardware is generally robust and reliable, though occasionally a component may need to be replaced or upgraded. You may also want to add a component such as a sound card or a LAN card.

When working with hardware you are unlikely to harm yourself or your equipment providing you follow a few simple guidelines.

The most basic of these is: always power down and disconnect from the mains power source before you remove any covers or lids. PCs run on AC mains power – they are no more (or less) dangerous than any other mains-powered household gadget.

Once the machine is disconnected from the power, you will need to remove the lid, cover, or side panel in order to access the inside of the machine. Covers and panels are usually secured by two or three screws with a 'star' style head. The best tool for removing them is a Phillips #2 screwdriver. (Occasionally, usually on older systems, you may still encounter torxx screws. In this case you will need to use a torxx driver.)

Having removed the screws, put them somewhere safe. Next, slide back and remove the lid, cover, or side panel of the machine. If you haven't done this before, the inside of the system probably looks quite formidable (see following figure). Don't panic – it's not half as complicated as it looks!

Before you touch any of the internal components, you should touch a bare metal section of the chassis of the machine. This safely discharges any static in your body – or at least equalizes it with any in the machine – so there is no difference of potential between you and the machine. Having discharged any static in this way, you should always touch bare metal before touching any component. Remember, even though you can't see static it can damage your system.

Wearing a wrist strap which you attach to the chassis of the PC means that you are permanently 'touching' bare metal.

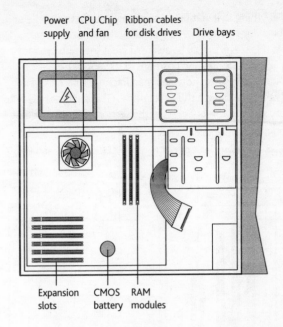

Power supply | CPU Chip and fan | Ribbon cables for disk drives | Drive bays

Expansion slots | CMOS battery | RAM modules

If you want a wrist strap, you can buy one for a few pounds from a local PC shop. Just remember NOT to wear it if you are in contact with high voltage equipment like a laser printer where it could conduct a high voltage to you rather than static away from you.

The main components

Motherboard

The motherboard – sometimes known as the main board, or system board – literally holds the other components together. You can think of it as the communications highway of the system. Every component communicates with the other components on the board through its communications channels, or buses. Like most PC hardware it's pretty tough and you are unlikely to need

to do anything to it. If it fails, you simply replace the whole unit.
The following figure shows a typical modern motherboard.

At this stage, simply be aware of what the motherboard
looks like and the size and positions of its various expansion
slots and sockets. Also note any manufacturer's name and
serial numbers, though this isn't critical. (There's an easy way to
identify your motherboard – see the section on RAM modules,
below.)

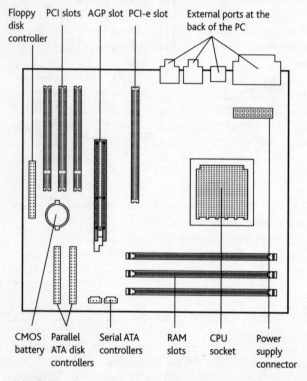

CPU

The CPU – Central Processing Unit – is often thought of
as being the 'brain' of the system, and sits in a socket on the
motherboard. Because of the heat generated when it is running,

it is fitted with a heat sink and a cooling fan. If the heat sink becomes clogged with dust or the fan doesn't work, your PC will overheat and stop working within a couple of minutes of being turned on.

RAM modules

These modules make up the main memory of the system. If you have one or more spare RAM slots on the board, then the most cost-effective upgrade you can do will be to add some more RAM. Most PCs bought from high street or online retailers ship with enough RAM to work, but can usually be improved by adding some more.

Because the major manufacturers of RAM are in the business of selling as much of the stuff as they can, they will make it as easy as possible for you to identify your system and its memory needs. The following figure shows the results from a free utility downloadable from www.crucial.com. Note that it also identifies your motherboard.

Disk drive controllers

The standard disk drive controller is the EIDE interface – also known as the parallel ATA interface. There are usually two of these on most motherboards. Each one has two rows of 20 pins and the surround to the pins usually has a slot so that the data cable which connects it to the drive can only be fitted one way. The cables themselves are usually round in section these days, but an older one may be a traditional ribbon cable. Ribbon cables have a red or pink stripe down one side – this indicates line 1. Where there are two controllers they are designated Primary and Secondary. Each controller supports two attached devices such as hard drives or CD/DVDs which are designated as either Master or Slave. Sometimes a primary controller is coloured red, blue or green to indicate that it is a higher speed type. This is not, however, an official standard and colours are often inconsistent.

Some newer systems may use Serial ATA (SATA) disk drives. The controllers for these are small rectangular connectors with just seven pins. It is possible to use a mix of SATA and parallel ATA drives, but it can lead to complications and is probably best avoided.

Power supply unit

The Power Supply Unit (PSU) converts alternating current (AC) mains power to direct current (DC) which the PC can use. The highest output voltage from the PSU is 12 volts, so nothing 'downstream' of it is likely to do you any harm. The unit itself, however, carries full mains power and should be treated with caution. A PSU is an example of what the trade calls a 'field replaceable module'. In other words, if it fails, replace it as a unit – don't try to open it and fix it – bin it and fit another one!

The outputs of the PSU are to one of three standard connectors. There is a small connector for floppy disk drives (a Berg connector), a Molex connector for other drives such as hard disks, CD-ROMs, etc., and SATA connectors for Serial ATA drives. Of these three power connector types, the Molex is the commonest. It is a general-purpose power connector and can be used to supply power to anything from disk drives to fans. Where a device doesn't have the appropriate connector there is usually an adaptor cable available, for example, you can attach a Serial ATA drive to a Molex connector by using a SATA to Molex adaptor cable. You can also buy splitter and extension cables to increase the number of available power supply connections.

Disk drives

Hard disk drives are usually 40-pin parallel ATA devices or, on newer systems, there may be 7-pin Serial ATA devices. The following figure shows a Serial ATA disk and connectors.

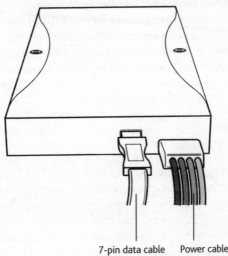

7-pin data cable   Power cable

Whichever type your system uses, it will need to be attached to an appropriate power line and a data cable. Power connectors are designed so that they will only fit one way and data cables are usually keyed so that they too, will only fit one way. Some older 40-pin cables may not be keyed, and the rule here is 'pink next to the power'. That is, the red or pink stripe down one side of the ribbon cable which indicates line 1 should be attached to the drive so that it is closest to the power connector.

CD and DVD drives – whether they are read only (ROM) drives or burners – are known collectively as optical drives because they work on laser light instead of the magnetic fields used by hard and floppy disk types. Even the fastest of these are relatively slow compared with magnetic hard drives, so they are frequently attached to the secondary EIDE/ATA controller, especially where this is the slower of the two controllers on the board.

Graphics

Most modern systems use the Accelerated Graphics Port (AGP) or a card in the later PCI-e slot to output information to the screen. An AGP card is normally fitted in a dedicated slot on the motherboard, brown in colour, and not aligned with the other expansion slots. These vary in size and orientation according to the type of AGP card on your system. The PCI-e slot (more below) is a general purpose slot which is frequently used for graphics cards but may also be used for other purposes such as gigabit Ethernet.

Many systems, especially budget systems from high street or online retailers, have on-board graphics – that is, a dedicated graphics chip connected directly to the motherboard. Most on-board graphics set-ups are suitable for relatively undemanding everyday applications like word processing, e-mail and browsing the Web. Sophisticated high-end games, or Computer Aided Design (CAD) packages may need a high-end graphics card in either an AGP or PCI-e expansion slot.

PCI expansion cards

Peripheral Component Interconnect (PCI) is the standard for most expansion cards on modern systems. The PCI slots on your motherboard are white (or off-white) and there are usually three or four of them. Any PCI card can be fitted in any PCI slot and – given the right drivers – will Plug and Play 'out of the box'.

A newer standard PCI-e (the 'e' is for 'Express') provides a means of connecting faster PCI-e expansion cards to your system. The PCI-e slot is normally the same colour as the standard PCI slots and is physically longer. There are also four different specifications with different sized slots. Smaller (i.e. lower-powered) cards will generally work in larger slots but the reverse is not the case even where a card physically fits in the slot. PCI-e is increasingly used as an alternative to the Accelerated Graphics Port (AGP) for graphics output, though it can be used to attach other card types such as high-speed LAN adapters.

CMOS battery

This is a small battery – like an oversized watch battery in appearance – which provides power to the CMOS while the system is turned off. These settings are kept live when the PC is turned off because the battery provides the necessary power. Rather like the battery on a car, it is recharged when the system is running and discharges when the system is turned off. Repeated charging and discharging will eventually cause the battery to fail. When this happens, a common symptom is that the PC loses track of the correct time. If this happens, then it's time to replace the CMOS battery. These can be bought for a couple of pounds from electronics or electrical goods shops. They are more or less standard components, but an easy way to make sure that you get the right thing is to power down the machine, remove the old battery and take it to the shop and ask for 'another of these'. When you return with your new battery, put it in the holder on the motherboard, replace the case cover on the PC and reboot it. As the machine reboots, press the key to enter the CMOS Setup screen (usually [Delete]) and check that your system has correctly identified the disk drives, etc. You can reset the time and date here as well, but it may be easier to leave time and date settings and correct them through the Control Panel later.

Why some things aren't worth upgrading

PCs become more powerful and cheaper with every year that passes, and each release of the operating system and other software requires more and better resources. For the first couple of years of your PC's life you can probably keep up with this – a couple of sticks of extra RAM will improve the performance of your PC from day one. You can add to the total RAM count without throwing anything away.

If your hard disk is starting to get full, you can probably fit a second disk to increase you total storage – again, adding capacity without throwing anything away. However, the case for upgrading other components, such as the CPU, is not so clear cut. Suppose, for example, you were to buy a new CPU chip that was (say) 20% faster than your existing chip.

* Is the chip compatible with other components on your system, especially the motherboard? Check with the motherboard manual and/or the manufacturer's website.
* Will the 20% faster chip result in a 20% increase in the overall performance of the system? The answer here is almost certainly 'No'.
* What do you do with the component you are replacing? Sell it? Throw it away?

In general, you need to ask yourself whether in a world of ever-decreasing hardware and system prices, an upgrade is worth the effort and cost of doing it compared with replacing the computer.

Replacement, on the other hand, may well be cost-effective particularly on a relatively new machine where a component has failed. If, for example, your CPU chip has failed, you have no choice but to abandon the old one. The cost calculation here is simply whether it will be better to fit a new chip – possibly even a slightly faster one, a sort of 'incidental upgrade' – or abandon the old system altogether and buy a new one. The decision is more to do with finance than technology as such.

Things to remember

* Always power down and disconnect before opening the case or removing any covers.
* Always discharge any static in your body by touching bare metal on the case before touching any components. Better still, use an anti-static wrist strap.

* Don't use a wrist strap when working with high voltage equipment such as laser printers.
* Some components become hot during normal operation. Handle them with care.
* PCI slots are universal – any PCI device will fit in any slot.
* PCI-e slots come in various lengths and not all devices are compatible with all slots of this type.
* Increasing the RAM installed on your system is a very cost-effective upgrade, particularly if you have any empty RAM slots.
* Not everything is worth upgrading, particularly if your system is more than a couple of years old.

6

preventive
maintenance

Preventive maintenance is the computer equivalent of cleaning the oven or weeding the garden; something that can always be postponed until 'tomorrow'. The best way to avoid this is to adopt a regular schedule, such as the one outlined in this chapter. The daily tasks can be scheduled to run automatically – just make sure that they are scheduled to run at a time when the computer will be turned on!

Working inside the case will require you to adopt the sort of safe working techniques outlined in Chapter 5 to prevent damage to components or yourself.

We also consider here the role of surge suppressors in protecting your system from mains voltage changes and how to dispose safely of old equipment.

A maintenance schedule

Preventive maintenance and cleaning are tedious but necessary if you want to keep your system running efficiently, and a regular maintenance schedule can save you time and money on maintenance and repair bills.

The key to effective maintenance is a regular pattern of work. Some tasks should be done daily, some weekly, some occasionally. Many routine tasks – such as backups and virus scans – can be automated through Windows.

Daily

* **Virus scan.** Your virus scanner should have the capability of running at a pre-set time each day. If you leave your system permanently on, you can schedule this for the small hours of the morning. Don't forget that the scanner needs to update its 'definitions' files, so schedule the update to run just before the scan. There's more on viruses in Chapter 8.
* **Spyware scan.** This complements the virus scan and ideally, it should be done immediately before or after the virus scan.
* **Backup.** It is prudent to back up your data daily. The minimum you should do is to back up data which has been modified (a differential backup) with a full data backup once a week.

Weekly

* Full data backup, preferably to a rotating disk (or tape) set.
* Defragment the hard disk (see Chapter 1).
* Run the Disk Cleanup Wizard (see Chapter 1).

Monthly

* Clean optical drives – CDROM/DVD – with a cleaner disk.
* Archive backup of data – store away from the PC.
* **Mouse.** If you are still using a 'ball' mouse, clean the rollers by scraping gently with a toothpick or similar.

* **Monitor.** Power down and clean the screen with a soft cloth or an anti-static wipe.
* Check the keyboard for sticky keys – clean with canned air if necessary.

On failure
* **Floppy disk drive.** The cleaning disk which you can use for cleaning floppy drives is mildly abrasive, so it should only be used sparingly to avoid long-term cumulative damage to the drive.

Yearly
* **Case.** Open the case. Remove dust deposits by brushing gently with a natural bristle brush, then blow out with canned air, or use a special PC vacuum cleaner.
* Adaptor cards, cables and removable components – clean contacts and reseat.

Ongoing/as required
* **CMOS.** Record and/or backup CMOS settings.
* **System.** Maintain a record of hardware, software and settings of the system. Don't forget your e-mail account settings, dialup numbers and passwords. Note all changes in a system notebook – that's 'notebook' in the old fashioned sense of a pen and paper record – it doesn't need mains power, batteries, or disk storage and there's a lot to be said for that!

Cleaning products and tools

Commonly used products and tools include:
* **Canned air.** Use this for blowing dust from awkward corners. Most PC shops sell it.
* **Natural fibre brushes.** A small paint brush or a pastry brush is ideal. Make sure, though, that it has natural bristles as some man-made fibres can generate static electricity which could damage components.

* **Antistatic wipes.** These are usually individually wrapped. They can be bought from most PC shops.
* **Denatured alcohol.** This can simply be a bottle of meths or surgical spirit which you can buy from a hardware shop or pharmacy. Alcohol cuts through grease very effectively and evaporates quickly.
* **Mild detergent solution.** Tap water with a squirt of washing-up liquid is a very good cleaning solution, especially for the outside of the case, etc. It needs to be used with care, of course, as water and electricity can be a hazardous combination. Don't apply the solution directly, use a dampened cloth and use sparingly.
* **Cleaning disks.** The cleaning disks which you use on a floppy drive are mildly abrasive and should be used with restraint. The cleaning disks/kits which you can use for CD or DVD drives are not generally abrasive and can be used as necessary or monthly as a routine preventive measure.
* **Cotton buds.** These are useful for general purpose cleaning. They can be used in conjunction with canned air and a natural bristle brush for mechanical removal of dirt and debris from awkward corners. They can also be dipped in alcohol for liquid cleaning where necessary.
* **Non-static vacuum cleaners.** These are small cleaners – often pistol grip in shape – which are intended for use with PCs. They need to be used with care as there is the possibility of damaging or dislodging components.

Before using any product on your PC, check that it is suitable for its intended use. For instance, if you plan on cleaning the case with a detergent solution or alcohol, apply it to a small area that is usually out of sight to check that it's okay.

In terms of Health and Safety law in the UK, there are regulations under the Control of Substances Hazardous to Health (COSHH) regulations, and in the USA all such products have a Material Safety Data Sheet (MSDS). You can check the nature of any product by searching on the Internet.

Cleaning

The case

Power down and 'wash' with a cloth that has been dipped in mild detergent solution and wrung out. Allow the cleaned surfaces to dry fully before reconnecting the power. For a really good job, you can follow detergent cleaning with a rub down with a cloth that has been moistened with alcohol. Again, allow the cleaned surface to dry fully before reconnecting the power.

Monitors

LCD – flat panel – monitors can be cleaned with a glass cleaner and a lint-free cloth. Don't spray the cleaner directly on to the screen, but apply a small amount to the cloth, then wipe the surface with it. LCD screens are easily scratched, so you should work gently. Be careful not to leave any excess on the screen and allow half an hour or so before powering up again.

Cathode ray tube (CRT) monitors – the ones that look like television sets – need to be treated with care. Even when they are turned off they contain very high voltages. Always disconnect the monitor before working on it and never wear a wrist strap or even metal jewellery that could come into contact with it.

A simple soap-and-water solution can be used for cleaning the outside of the case and the screen itself. Don't use excessive amounts of the solution: dip the cleaning cloth in it, then wring out until it is damp but has no excess moisture. Clean the monitor and dry it with a clean cloth before powering up. Don't use commercial cleaners or aerosol sprays other than those specifically designed for use with monitors.

With either type of monitor, power up when you have finished and the screen is dry, then check that any controls for brightness, alignment, etc. are okay. It's quite easy to knock a control accidentally during cleaning and to lose the 'picture' as a result.

Inside the case

Dust is an ever present problem with computer systems. The components generate static charges as a by-product of their operation, and the various cooling fans draw air (and dust) into the case. Over time, the accumulation of dust can be sufficient to cause overheating, so an annual spring clean of the interior of the case can be a useful investment of your time.

As with all work on the inside of the system box, power down and disconnect from the mains before removing the covers or side panels.

The first line of defence against accumulated dust is a small paint brush, or a pastry brush, with natural bristles which will not induce static in the components to which it is applied. Simply use the brush to dislodge accumulated dust – particularly on the CPU heat sink/fan assembly and the power supply fan. The loosened dust can be blown away using canned air or removed with a non-static vacuum cleaner.

While you have the case open, it is a good time to check that all of the fans rotate freely and are properly connected to the power connectors on the motherboard – it's quite easy to dislodge connection during the cleaning process. This is also a good time to replace any missing covers from unused expansion slots. This will help to optimize the airflow in the case and to keep atmospheric dust out.

Before replacing the cover or side panel, connect the machine to the mains and power up. Check that all fans – particularly the CPU fan – are working. A non-functioning CPU fan will cause the chip to overheat and the system will lock up in under a minute. Longer than a minute is sufficient to cause permanent damage so this is a check worth making.

Contacts and connections

This is not really necessary where a system is functioning properly, but some people like to clean and reseat internal components as part of their annual maintenance. If components have been handled and fitted properly – that is, contacts and edge connectors have never been touched by hand – then there is not likely to be any corrosion or oxidation to the surface.

If you do find it necessary to clean edge connectors on expansion cards or memory modules, then remove the module and use a very fine emery cloth or a specialist electrical contact cleaner spray. The easiest method is to use a pencil eraser to brush the contacts. When doing this, always work from the inner to the outer edge of the module to avoid peeling back the edge connectors.

Other internal components which fit into slots or sockets on the motherboard may work themselves loose over time. The repeated cycle of heating and cooling causes repeated expansions and contractions of the components which can cause them to work loose in their sockets – a phenomenon known as 'chip creep'. As a preventive measure, it may be prudent to remove and reseat any such components to establish a fresh electrical contact.

Removable media devices

Removable drives such as tape drives, floppy drives, CDs, DVDs, etc. are open to the air, and the media themselves are physically handled. This means that they can collect dust and finger grease which can be transferred from the disk to the drive heads. An indirect form of preventive maintenance, then, is to exercise care when handling removable media.

Magnetic media, floppy disks and tapes, etc., can easily be corrupted if they are stored close to strong magnetic fields, so you should avoid storing them near anything with an electric motor – like a vacuum cleaner – or anything with strong electro-magnetic fields such as CRT monitors or speakers.

When it comes to cleaning drives themselves, there are two approaches: removal and manual cleaning or using cleaning tapes or disks. Generally speaking, floppy drives are now so cheap that it may be cost-effective to replace then rather than spend time on cleaning them, though cleaning kits are available.

Optical drives – CD and DVD – as well as tape drives may be removed, stripped down and cleaned with alcohol and a lint-free cloth.

A cotton bud dipped in meths is an easy way to clean a lens. As an alternative, there are cleaning disks and kits available for most drive types. Optical media are mechanically 'swept' clean by brush heads mounted on a cleaning disk which passes over the laser lens. This is a non-destructive process. Cleaners for magnetic media are generally mildly abrasive so, whilst they are effective at removing the build-up of contaminants on the drive heads, excessive use can shorten the life of the drive.

Ventilation, dust and moisture control

Fortunately, PCs do best in the same sort of conditions that most of us find comfortable: not too hot, not too cold, moderate humidity and no sources of dust. Most domestic users will have no problems, but air conditioning systems can sometimes lower humidity to sub-optimal levels.

When you are carrying out preventive maintenance inside the case, look out for unusual patterns in the (inevitable) build-up of dust in the case as these may indicate missing expansion slot covers or cracks in the case.

Safety

Surge suppressors

Mains electrical supplies are subject to interruptions, voltage 'sags' and occasional 'spikes'. In commerce and industry, key machines are often protected by various technologies such as line conditioners and uninterruptible power supplies. For most home users, these technologies are disproportionate and expensive. However, a simple surge suppressor costs only a few pounds and will provide basic protection against power surges in the mains supply which could otherwise damage your system. If you don't have a surge suppressor – buy one!

Safe disposal of old equipment

Nearly everything inside a computer seems to be toxic and there are increasing levels of concern by government and local authorities about safe disposal. Before disposing of any piece of equipment it is wise to enquire about current legal requirements for the country, county or state where you live.

Batteries contain many toxic substances and need to be disposed of through a recognized disposal facility. They should never be incinerated or thrown out with household rubbish. Batteries which are damaged, or which leak, present a hazard to anyone handling them – be especially careful not to get electrolyte in your eyes.

Monitors – particularly CRT monitors – contain many toxic substances and may contain potentially lethal voltages even when they have been turned off for some time. They are subject to ever-tightening disposal regulations and you should find a specialist disposal facility.

Toner cartridges, refill kits and old ink jet cartridges may also need special disposal. However, many of these items are refillable and/or recyclable. Empty laser toner cartridges may even be saleable.

If you are in any doubt about the nature of any component or substance that you have to dispose of, then a search of the Internet for the UK Control of Substances Hazardous to Health (COSHH) regulations or the US counterpart Material Safety Data Sheet (MSDS) will give an indication of what is appropriate and/or legally required.

7

the Internet and e-mail

In this chapter we will look at a couple of popular ways of connecting to the Internet using either a broadband modem or a router. We will also look at how the Windows firewall can help to protect your system from intruders by restricting access to the net to those programs that you have decided are safe. Anti virus protection is considered at some length in Chapter 8.

For e-mail services we will consider both web-based services like Hotmail or Googlemail and the alternative pop3/smtp-based services that use e-mail software clients such as Windows Live Mail (which is basically a re-badged version of Outlook Express), Thunderbird or Pegasus.

You may find it helpful to look back at Chapter 4 when reading the e-mail section.

How to set up your Internet connection

Connecting to the Internet – for surfing, shopping, online banking, sending and receiving e-mails – is one of the main uses for the Home PC.

Before you start

In order to connect to the Internet you need some form of access account with an Internet Service Provider (ISP) and a physical connection through a modem or a router. To set up your Internet connection you will need an active account with your ISP, who will have provided you with a user name and a password – make sure you have these to hand.

Many ISPs provide a broadband modem as part of their broadband package. If this is the case, check that you have all the necessary cables and connectors and that you have read any installation instructions that come with it.

If you have bought your own modem (or router) you should also check any documentation that came with it. This chapter will take you through the setup process for equipment of this type though details may vary between specific products.

Settings and equipment check

As with all equipment installation you should check that you have all necessary cables and connectors and that you have read any instructions from the manufacturer. You will need to know some settings which will be provided by your ISP. These are:

* User name: yourusername@yourisp
* Password: nnnnnnn.

(These are needed for all connections including dialup.)

Other settings you may need for your router/broadband modem.

* Encapsulation: PPPoA
* Multiplexing: VC Based
* VPI: 0
* VCI: 38.

(Note: these are UK settings – if you are not in the UK, they may be different in your country/region.)

You don't need to know what these settings mean – just have them to hand and enter them when – or if – necessary.

Installing a USB broadband modem

The most popular way of connecting to the Internet is through some form of broadband connection – this is also known as an Asymmetric Digital Subscriber Line (ADSL) connection.

The modem used in this example is a cheap generic one based on a chip set from Lucent Technologies.

Before you start

1 Unpack the modem and check the cables and connectors are all present and correct.
2 Make sure that you have all connection details provided by your ISP to hand (see the section Settings and Equipment Check above).
3 Check that you have the manufacturer's driver CD.
4 Read any documentation. In this instance, for example, you are warned not to allow Windows to Plug and Play the new modem but to insert the driver CD and install the manufacturer's drivers.
5 Don't plug the modem into the USB port yet. You will be prompted later.

The installation

1 Put the driver CD in the CD/DVD drive and navigate to the setup program for your system. NB: Do not let it autorun when Windows detects it.

2 Click on the setup.exe file to run it. Skip over the Unknown Publisher warning from Windows.

3 Accept the Licence Agreement and click on **Next** until you reach the Communication Settings page.

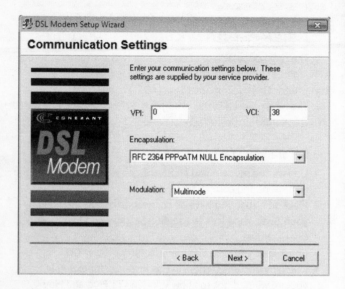

4 Enter the communications settings provided by your ISP then click on **Next**. After a final check that the settings are correct click on **Next** again to start the installation of the drivers.

5 As the installation proceeds you will receive another Unknown Publisher warning from Windows. Choose the Install Anyway option. You will be prompted to plug the modem into the USB port. Connect the modem and click on **Next**.

6 When the installer prompts you to reboot, click on the **Close** button.

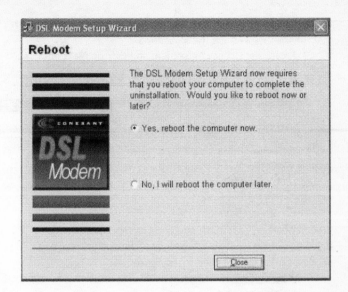

7 After the reboot, click on the connection icon and enter your user name and password to access your broadband account.

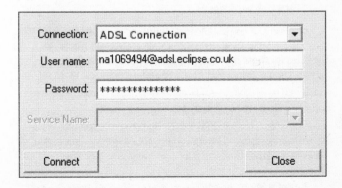

In this example we have walked through the installation of a 'typical' ADSL modem. Your modem will probably be different in some of its details so read the supplier's documentation before you start.

Installing a broadband modem/router

An increasingly popular way of connecting to the Internet is through a combined broadband modem/router. These are standalone devices which are permanently connected to the Internet even when your PC is turned off. They often provide wireless network connectivity as well, and are ideal for use with a small home network – whether wired, wireless, or both.

The example that follows assumes that you have a working Ethernet port on your machine – most modern machines do. If you don't have a network connection – for an RJ45 plug or a wireless card – you will need to install one.

In this chapter we will look at how to set up a modem/router through the browser on a single PC.

In order to do this, it's useful for you to know a couple of things about network addresses.

Network addresses

A network address is a series of numbers, like a phone number, which identifies a node such as a PC or a router on a network. The rules for these numbers are part of the Internet Protocol and are known as Internet Protocol addresses. This is invariably shortened to IP address. An IP address consists of four groups of numbers, separated by full stops.

192.168.2.1 – is a typical private IP address. Private addresses are reserved for use on private networks – like home networks – rather than the public addresses used on the (public) Internet.

Just as a phone number may consist of an exchange code and the individual's phone number, an IP address has two parts. In the case of a typical Class C address that you will use for home networking, the first three groups of numbers are the network part of the address and the last group indicates the computer, or router, or other device attached to that network. The address 192.168.2.1, then indicates device number 1 on the network indicated by 192.168.2.

Before you start

Check that you have all equipment and documentation (as in previous examples). You will also need to know the router's default IP address and its default user name and password. This information will be in its manual or setup instructions The default IP address in this example is 192.168.2.1 – this may be different if you are using a different make or model of router/modem.

Connecting your router

1 Connect all cables. There will be one from the Ethernet port on your PC to one of the ports on the router, and another from the router to the splitter which connects it and the phone to the phone line. Connect the router to its power supply. Various lights on the router will flicker as it runs through its power-on self-test/boot sequence.

2 When the router has settled down you will have an indicator to show that it is powered up along with other indicators for the ADSL side of the connection. The port to which you have connected the Ethernet cable should have a steady light to show that it is in place. Ports which have no cable attached will not show lights. If there are any problems at this stage – unlikely – then check cable connections and power and have a look at the router manual or setup instructions.

3 The next thing to do is to configure the modem/router through its web interface. To do this, start your web browser and type in the default IP address of your router. You don't

need 'http' or 'www' – just type the numeric IP address in the Address bar and press [Enter].

4 The browser will add the http://prefix for you and you will be taken to the login screen for the router. As this is the first time you have accessed the router there won't be a password in place – or if there is, it will be a default password from the manufacturer which will be shown in the documentation. The login screen will look something like this:

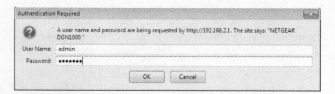

5 Enter a password – if necessary – and press [Enter]. The Welcome screen will list various options, including a setup wizard. You can use the wizard to enter the necessary information to set up your connection. For purposes of this example we will walk through the stages manually.

6 The first page to complete is Basic Settings.
   Here you need to enter:
   * Encapsulation method. Choose from the drop-down list.
   * Your login/user name – provided by your ISP.
   * Your password – probably provided by your ISP to begin with but which you can later change through their site.
   Unless you have good reason to do so, you should leave the other options at their default values. When you have checked the accuracy of the information click on the **Apply** button at the bottom of the screen. Don't bother with the **Test** button yet; this is a new set up and there is more information to be entered – the ADSL settings required by your ISP.

7 Click on the ADSL entry in the menu then enter the information supplied by your ISP in the fields on the form.

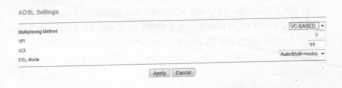

Click on the **Apply** button when your are finished.

8 Return to the Basic Setting page (see step 6) and click on the **Test** button. Initially this may report a failure but after a few seconds (if you have entered all the information correctly) it will report success.

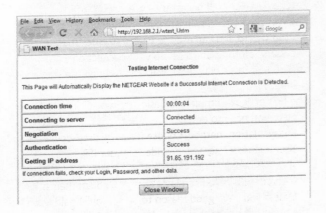

9 Click on the **Close Window** button. The router will need to reboot in order to save your settings – this may take half a minute or so.

10 In order to test your router, point your browser at a website and check that it loads okay.

The Windows firewall

An additional level of protection is given by controlling which programs on your PC can access the Internet. Obviously, your web browser and e-mail programs need to be given access. Other programs can be given access to the Internet if you allow them.

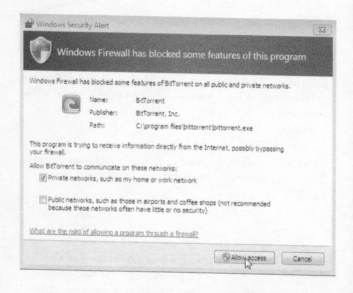

The screenshot shows a program attempting to access the Internet and being intercepted by the Windows firewall. If you wish to give this program access, click on the **Allow Access** button. Choosing the **Cancel** button will leave it blocked. In order to check or modify access through the Windows firewall navigate to **Control Panel > System and Security > Windows firewall > Allow a program** ..... You will see a list of programs like this:

Allow programs to communicate through Windows Firewall

To add, change, or remove allowed programs and ports, click Change settings.

What are the risks of allowing a program to communicate?

Change settings

Allowed programs and features:

Name	Home/Work (Private)	Public
☑ avgemc.exe	☑	☐
☑ avgnsx.exe	☑	☐
☑ avgupd.exe	☑	☐
☐ Connect to a Network Projector	☐	☐
☑ Core Networking	☑	☑
☐ Distributed Transaction Coordinator	☐	☐
☑ Dropbox	☑	☐
☑ File and Printer Sharing	☑	☑
☑ HomeGroup	☑	☐
☐ iSCSI Service	☐	☐
☐ Media Center Extenders	☐	☐
☐ Netlogon Service	☐	☐

By default this is a read-only list. If you want to change the settings of a program you need to click on the **Change Settings** button before changing the checkbox(es) next to the program in the list.

How e-mail works

E-mail is one of the most widely used features of the Internet. We generally take it for granted these days that we can communicate more or less instantly with anyone in the world through e-mail. For the home user, there are two e-mail types – web-based services or POP3 services with addresses like yourname@yourisp.com.

Web-based services require you to log on to a site where you have an e-mail account and everything is done whilst logged on to that site. Probably the best known web-based mail service is Microsoft's Hotmail, though there are many alternative services such gmx.com or fastmail.fm.

POP3 services allow you to use a mail program such Windows Live Mail or Thunderbird. These are all programs – known as mail clients – which allow you to compose mail off-line, then connect to the Internet to send your messages and download any that you have received.

Sending and receiving POP3 e-mails means using two e-mail protocols – the Post Office Protocol – version 3 (POP3), which is used for receiving e-mails and the Simple Mail Transfer Protocol (SMTP), which is used for sending messages from your PC. In order to set up your e-mail client, you don't need to know anything about these mail protocols other than their names. What you do need to know, of course, is the names and addresses of the servers that use these protocols, along with your user name and password.

Chapter 4 explains how to find (or enter) the e-mail settings needed to make your e-mail system work. The illustrations are of the Windows Live Mail client as this is the most popular e-mail program with home users. It is not, however, difficult to apply the information given to other mail client programs. Just remember that you need two server addresses – possibly with the same password for each – a POP3 server for receiving incoming mail and an SMTP server for sending mail.

Things to remember

* Before setting up your Internet connection make sure that you have all the necessary settings from your ISP.
* Always check cabling and connectors for hardware before you start.
* If you are installing a modem – dialup or ADSL – make sure that you have the necessary drivers. If you don't have an installation CD you may need to visit the manufacturer's website (possibly on a different machine) and download them.

* A router has a built-in firewall and is therefore more secure than using a modem connection.
* The Windows firewall will block all new programs by default unless you decide otherwise.
* You can change your Windows firewall settings and program access through the Control Panel.
* A firewall does NOT protect you against viruses. You will need a separate virus scanner. Chapter 8 covers viruses and malware.

8

viruses and other malware

Viruses are probably the biggest single threat to Windows systems so the bulk of this chapter will take you through installing and configuring a popular anti-virus package from AVG. There are other free products such as Avast or Panda which deliver much the same functionality.

You may also come across free 'scanning' services online. Whilst some of these may be genuine, some of them are in fact malware exploits that will compromise your system; *treat them with great caution*.

We will also look at Windows Defender – which is part of Windows 7 – and some of the security features of the standard Windows browser Internet Explorer 8.

We also consider, briefly, Parental Control features of Windows 7 which you can use to filter unsuitable Internet content.

Basic precautions

To keep your PC safe from attack you should download and install any security updates from Microsoft. Don't forget that if you have reinstalled Windows you will have lost all your accumulated security downloads and will have to download and install them again.

Installing and using anti-virus software

The single most important tool for dealing with virus threats is an anti-virus software package. This needs to be installed and regularly updated. Most packages can be configured to update themselves regularly and this may happen a couple of times a week. An out-of-date virus scanner is worse than useless – it will not protect you from the ever-evolving pool of viruses but will make you think that you are protected when you are not!

There are many anti-virus packages available and they have many similarities with each other. One of the most effective and easy to use is AVG from Grisoft. They offer a number of packages for various sizes and types of business – more importantly for the home user, they offer a free version for private use. Check that you are eligible to use the free version – if you are a private household wishing to protect a single PC you almost certainly are – then download and install the free package. If you are not eligible to use the free version – you have more than one PC or your PC is attached to a network – you should visit www.grisoft.com and check on the licensing of their paid-for products and trial versions. You can also download a reference guide and an installation guide from their site.

To find out more about AVG Free Edition and AVG Trial Versions visit http://free.grisoft.com.

Installing the anti-virus package – whether AVG or other – is no different from installing any other piece of software on your system. Make sure that you have sufficient rights – you'll need Administrator rights – and click on the installer file icon to start the process. Follow the on-screen instructions until the installer has finished running – you may have to reboot the system at some point. The example which follows is of AVG Free edition – illustrations courtesy of Grisoft sro, Czech Republic.

Installing AVG free edition

1 The AVG installer has the company logo on its icon. In order to install AVG you will need Administrator privileges, so right-click on the installer icon and select **Run as Administrator** from the context menu.

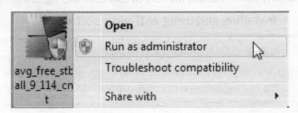

2 Skip over the security warning from Windows, choose your language from the drop-down menu (the default is English) then click on the **Next** button to proceed. You will be presented with at choice to install either the free product or a trial version of the full product. Make your choice and click on the appropriate link, then on the **Next** button. (For purposes of this example this will be the free version). The installer will now spend a couple of minutes downloading the installation files.

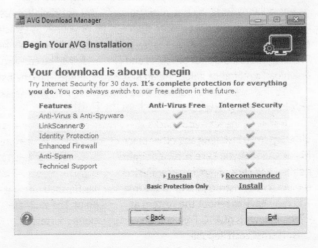

3 Read the Licence Agreement, tick the box to say that you have done this, then click on the **Accept** button to proceed.

4 At the next screen you will be given the choice between a Standard installation (the default) or Custom installation. Choose the Standard installation and click on **Next**. At the next screen, confirm your user name and accept the assigned licence number, then click on **Next**.

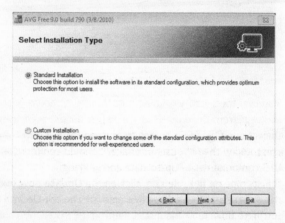

5 You will now be given the opportunity to install some optional extras. Make your selection(s) and click on the **Next** button to proceed. The installer will now spend several minutes copying files and configuring your system. There is a **Cancel** button if you change your mind but apart from this there is nothing for you to do but watch until the Installer confirms that it has finished. When this happens, click on the **Finish** button.

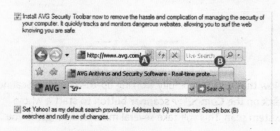

6 With the installation complete the next stage is to Optimize Scanning Performance. This can be deferred if you wish, but for purposes of this worked example we will click on the recommended **Optimize scanning now** option. This may take several minutes; the exact length of time depends, of course, on your particular hardware resources.

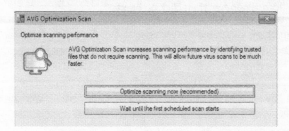

7 Once the initial scan is complete, click on the **System Tray** icon to open the AVG user interface. It should confirm that all AVG components are up-to-date and working.

Just to be on the safe side, click on the **Update now** button and if there are any updates available click on the **Update** button to download and install them.

8 Now that you have a fully working up-to-date virus scanner, click on the **Computer scanner** button to start a whole system scan. This will take several minutes – longer if you

have a lot of files. With luck, you will receive an all clear
message. If not, follow the instructions on screen.

Scheduling updates and scans

Whatever anti-virus package you have installed, you need to
consider how to organize regular updates and system scans that fit
in with your pattern of PC use and your type of Internet connection.
Again, this is illustrated by reference to AVG Free, though similar
procedures should be available in any other anti-virus package that
you may choose.

If you have an always-on broadband connection you can
schedule updates for times when you won't be actually working on
the PC, with a system scan scheduled to run after any update.

Scheduling updates

1 Open the AVG interface by clicking on its icon in the System
Tray then click on the **Overview** button from the menu on
the left.

2 Click on the Update Manager icon (bottom right).

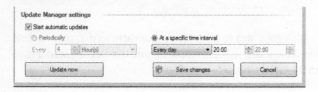

3 You can choose to Update Now. More importantly for
our present purposes you can specify the time of day and
frequency of updates. Make your choices and click on the
Save changes button.

Scheduling scans

1 Open the AVG interface by clicking on its icon in the System
Tray then click on the **Computer scanner** button from the
menu on the left.

2 Click on the **Schedule Scans** icon (bottom right).
3 Click on the **Edit scan schedule** button and make your choices:
4 Click on **Save** to save your new settings then exit from the AVG interface.

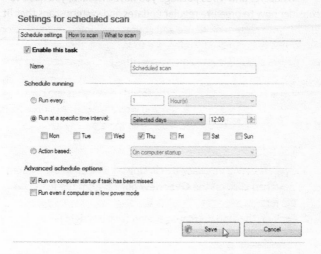

It's a good idea to schedule your updates so that they run just before your scans, so that you can be sure that you are scanning with the latest virus definition files.

Windows Defender

Windows Defender is part of Windows 7 but it is not turned on by default when Windows is installed. You need to turn it on and to configure it.

1 To turn Defender on, search on 'defender' in the Search box on the **Start** menu and select Windows Defender from the resulting list. You will see a notification like this. Click on the link to start Defender.

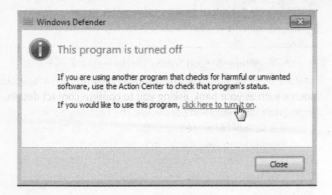

2 Click on the Scan tool to run a quick scan.

3 Choose **Tools** from the main menu, then **Options**. You can now schedule scans and default actions for Defender. These settings are similar to those for your virus scanner. Unless you disable it, Windows Defender will now start whenever you boot to Windows and will run in the background to protect you from malware.

Other spyware and ad-ware detection packages

Windows Defender is not the only tool available for spyware and ad-ware detection and removal. There are several other packages – such as Lavasoft's AdAware or Spybot Search and Destroy which can be downloaded free for personal use.

SmartScreen Filter in Internet Explorer 8

Phishing (pronounced 'fishing') is the increasingly common practice of sending e-mails which appear to come from a reputable source such as your bank, asking you to confirm contact details, login information or even passwords. The best way to avoid trouble is simply to delete any suspicious e-mails. However, as an extra layer of precaution, Internet Explorer 8 ships with SmartScreen Filter to combat phishing attacks. Like Defender this is not turned on by default at install time. In order to fix this:

1 Start Internet Explorer.

2 Click on the **Safety** button (top right).

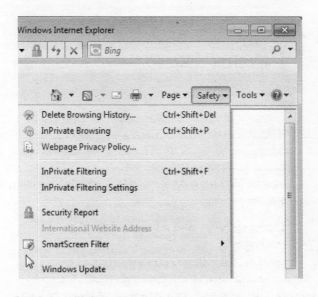

3 Click on the **SmartScreen Filter** entry in the drop-down menu.

4 Now that it is activated SmartScreen Filter will:

* Check websites against a list of reported phishing and malware sites.
* Check software downloads against a list of reported malware sites.
* Warn you if you visit known phishing websites and other websites that may contain malware that may lead to identity theft.

5 If there is a problem with a site you will see a warning like this:

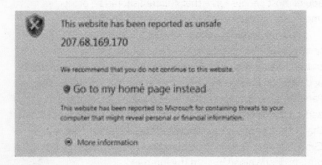

InPrivate browsing

This is another security feature built in to Internet Explorer 8.

Normally, when you visit a website Explorer keeps a record of where you have been (a history list) and will accept cookies from sites so that they can identify you when you return to them. Some sites contain links to other sites and these too may be tracked usually for legitimate reasons. However, there are times – such as when you are using a public computer – when you don't want this information to be recorded and stored. InPrivate browsing gives you the option to turn off these features for the current session ONLY. To activate the service choose the InPrivate Filtering entry from the Safety menu in Internet Explorer or press [Control] + [Shift] + [F]. When you exit from the browser session you will have left no trail of your activities for that session and the browser will resume its earlier settings next time it is started.

Parental control software

There is no censorship on the World Wide Web – no one owns it or controls it – and for the most part that is beneficial to all of us. However, it does mean that there are some pretty unpleasant websites varying from the salacious to the downright perverted, and no matter what we may think about freedom of expression for adults most people agree that children should be protected from undesirable web content.

As with spyware and ad-ware, public perception of the problems of pornography, violence or racism on the Net, has led to the development of software tools to deal with the problems, and to restrict access to sites which you regard as unsuitable. Parental control software has been available as a third-party add-on for several years. These tend to be reasonably priced rather than free. Two of the best known of these are Net Nanny and Cyber Sentinel. These can be bought on disk from some retail outlets or downloaded from the Internet.

The Parental Controls in Windows 7 are sufficient for most users. You can set them up through the Control Panel.

Notes

Notes _____

Notes